John Stuart

Their first meeting –
shaking the hand
he would come to hold

Double Vision

A SECOND LOOK AT LIFE

Verse by John Stuart

Illustrations by Bill Goodburn

Diplopia Books

Published by
DIPLOPIA BOOKS
Whiteknowe
Innerleithen Road
Peebles EH45 8BD

A catalogue record for this book is available
from the British Library.

ISBN: 978-0-9559010-0-3

Typeset in Golden Cockerel
Designed by Mark Blackadder

Printed and bound by
Kelso Graphics
The Knowes, Kelso TD5 7BH

Contents

Foreword

Double Vision brings out the humour of day-to-day events by the use of three-line verses and sketches. These verses, which are written in haiku-senryu style, reveal unexpected or amusing aspects of the commonplace. These aspects are often lost in the hustle of modern life. The popularity of haiku-senryu verse lies in the imagery they provide within a few syllables. Their use of imagination, some irony, lateral thinking, or just a play on words, gives an insight (or double vision) which adds to the moment.

Double Vision

VIII

Haiku are of Japanese origin and traditionally arranged in three lines of five, seven and five syllables respectively. They are written to capture the essence of a moment or experience and often describe nature. Senryu verses are a variant; they have the same syllabic structure but tend more to ironic observations on human nature. The distinction between haiku and senryu is, however, not absolute. Both types of verse often have a subtlety and significance that require a moment's reflection. Brevity (less is more) is their essence and verses written in English, which has longer syllables than the Japanese language, often have fewer syllables than traditional Japanese haiku.

Double Vision has been written for the reader to sample and return to, rather than to read as a continuum, and the verses are arranged under subject headings to encourage this. These verses have a cheerful or wry approach to life events (human and animal) and lighten the more serious moments. Many will require a pause for thought and may give satisfaction once the 'twist' (double vision) is worked out.

Illustrating the haiku are pen-and-ink sketches which contain their own humour and which complement the verses. For those haiku without a sketch, readers are asked to create their own images which is part of the fun of reading haiku.

The Authors

The authors live in the Scottish Borders and have a background of medicine (John Stuart) and law (Bill Goodburn). More importantly, by not taking things at their face value, they share a delight in finding the humour or alternative meaning that can lie behind daily events. Their respective interests in writing haiku and sketching with pen and ink have come together in this book to show that not everything is what it seems when you view life in *Double Vision.*

Acknowledgements

An early draft of this book was made possible by the computing skills of Professor Iain Percy-Robb and was then displayed to guests at Balgonie Country House Hotel in Ballater by John and Cilla Finnie and Moira McDougall. Encouragement and essential feedback was also provided by our wives (Gillian and Ann), our children, and many friends.

We are indebted to all of the above who laughed or groaned at our humour. We hope that most of the groans have been removed. Finally, much of the charm of a book lies in its layout and design for which we thank Mark Blackadder.

Wistful memories –
when their glasses
were full

❖

In Love

Twin-bedded room
tonight, my wife
no push over

⁘

Her first kiss –
staring cross-eyed
at the politician

⁘

Song of lost love –
played on
her heartstrings

⁘

Two heads
on the pillow –
better than one

⁘

Walking alone
he made room for her
beside him

⁘

Aware of each other
across the crowded room
radar full on

⁘

Their first meeting –
shaking the hand
he would come to hold

⁘

Moles in the meadow
subterranean amour
making the earth move

⁘

The nearness of you
an old melody
playing in his head

⁘

Love at first sight –
their eyes met
a tail wagged

⁘

She brushed against him
static electricity
or something else?

⁘

Loving her
more than chocolate cake
he tried another slice

⁘

Head over heels –
losing his balance
over her

⁘

Lost for a shipmate
lonely mariner
all at sea

❖

Inside him
the fire she lit those years ago
still burning

❖

Muzzle to the ground
cartographer of lamp-posts
canine A to Z

⁘

Animal Life

My thirsty dog
making empty gestures
at lamp-posts

❖

Desperate
for a tree –
the old hound

❖

Dinner guests
the house dog stretches –
it's time to go

❖

Terrier excavating –
making a mountain
out of a molehill

⁘

Face of the old dog
looking like its owner
which came first?

⁘

Butcher's shop –
window shopping
the labrador drools

⁘

'Beware of the dog'
behind the gate
the lonely spaniel

⁘

Strutting her stuff
feline fur
on the catwalk

⁘

Animal Life

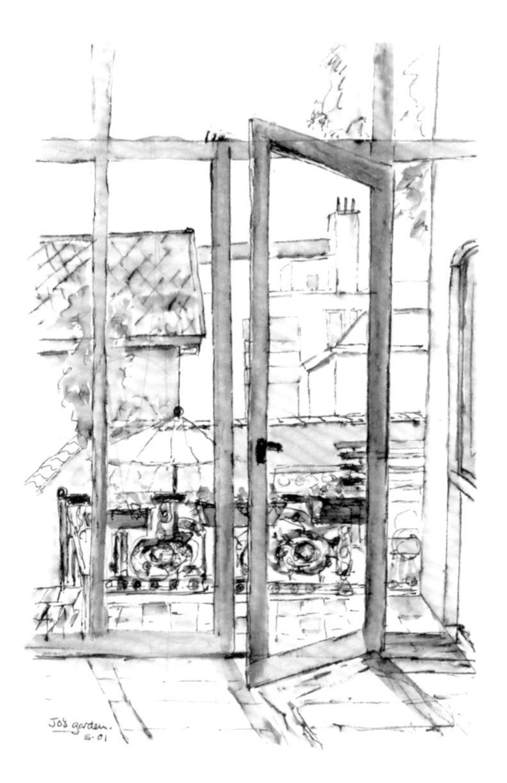

Balcony door ajar
stealthily to the kitchen
cat burglar

❖

Rabbit on the road
feathered friend
crowing over dinner

⁘

Bird Life

Perched above the road
crows expectant
their fast-food chain

⁘

Cuckoo clock
timely shelter
for a frequent flyer

⁘

Robin
on a spade –
site foreman

⁘

Timber-framed house
distant echo
of a woodpecker

❖

No fish today?
river heron on one leg
scratching his head

❖

The fish motionless –
eyeing the heron
eyeing the fish

❖

Too-early alarm
crows on my fence
a stone's throw

✣

Mountain echo
of a cuckoo –
calling itself

✣

Nightfall –
silent beaks
tucked underwing

✣

Bagpipes for ever –
Scots blowing
their own trumpet

⁘

Scotland

Scottish Parliament
foot of the Royal Mile
head of a nation

⁘

The warmth of Scotland –
triumph of man
over climate

⁘

Scottish hospitality –
taken
as given

⁘

Whisky distillery –
still the taste
of Scotland

❖

Distillery –
mashing malted barley
to sow wild oats

❖

Scottish morning
porridge on the Aga –
central heating

❖

Bull in a field
Scots' right to roam –
horns of a dilemma

⁘

Southern Upland Way
stepping out in Buchan land
moorland pursuit

⁘

Keeping up his roar –
stag on the hill
in a rut

⁘

Yellow broom
sweeping
over Scottish hillside

⁘

Burns Supper
an offal stomach
addressed in good spirit

Birthday fortitude
spirit undiluted
the essence of Scotland

Tossing the caber –
chief upset of
the Highland Games

Scottish loch
surface ripples
nothing monstrous

❖

Specialization –
my Apple Mac
her Whisky Mac

❖

Horologist's
hourly
earache

❖

Time Passes

Antique clock –
old timer
still ticking over

⁘

Life's clock ticking on
minutes to make the most of
no second time

⁘

Stressed-oak table
looking older than its years
my wife feeling it

⁘

Short-term memory loss
how did I start
this haiku?

✣

Familiar face –
the name
no longer

✣

Forty year reunion
familiar images
moving more slowly

✣

Her wedding ring
worn thinner
than her patience

✣

Now white-haired
my barber reminisces
when I was grey

✣

Climbing days over
old boot on the window sill
geranium pot

❖

Happy to be old –
being a survivor
can't take that away!

❖

Young girl
smiling sweetly
I look over my shoulder

⁘

Time marches on –
a procession
of old memories

⁘

Old town cinema –
movie memories
flickering past

⁘

My hairdresser
making the most of it –
splitting hairs

Old age –
knocking the stuffing
out of her shape

⁘

Abandoned horsebox
childhood memories –
of horseplay

⁘

Playful granddaughter
helping him enjoy
another childhood

⁘

Growing older
getting younger –
joie de vivre

⁘

Memory bank
full of interest
from old transactions

⁘

Still life
in the art gallery –
old man sleeping

❖

Art

Eye of the artist
seeing a face
getting behind it

❖

Art exhibitions –
always, on my favourite,
a red dot

❖

Creative artist
breathing life into still-life
mid-wife of her art

❖

Cut flowers in a vase
immortalised on canvas
before they all die

❖

Freeing the mind
to soar over landscapes –
picture gallery

❖

Suffering for his art –
snowscape watercolourist
painting with icicles

❖

Art gallery –
looking good
for your money

❖

Art

29

Bicycle handlebars
horns of Picasso's goat
art of recycling

⁘

Candlelight concert
the composer
dimly recognised

Music

Anxious musician
composing –
her mind

❖

Concert hall
acoustically tuning
the space around the notes

❖

Pop musician
striking a chord –
the audience rises

❖

Autobiography
of the jazz musician –
blowing his own trumpet

❖

Elevator
muzak
not uplifting

❖

Pianist
improvising
all that jazz

❖

Cold King Wenceslas
keeping a lookout
for winter fuel

❖

Accordionist
and his squeeze –
plaisir d'amour

⁘

Moonlight serenade
me and my shadow –
duetting

⁘

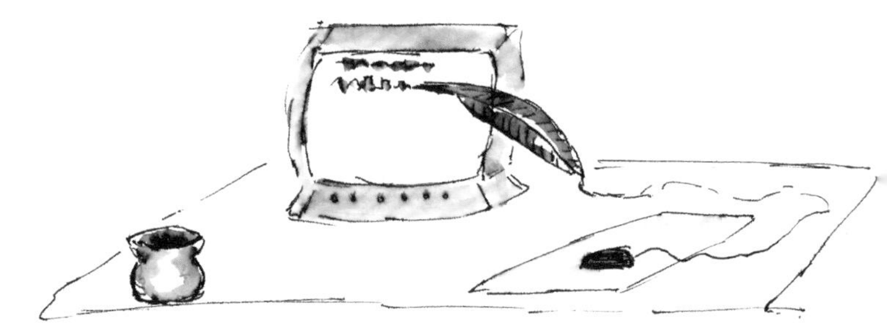

Pewter inkwell –
waiting for a quill pen
and a technophobe

⁘

The Writer

Blank sheet of paper –
stimulating the mind
more than the printed page

✣

Author at his desk
intellectual frenzy –
quietly writing

✣

Haiku writer
terse man
few words

✣

Publisher's deadline
writer's block
putting his head on it

❖

Master weaver
spinning a yarn
into a best seller

❖

Writer in his den
hiding from the world
creating another

❖

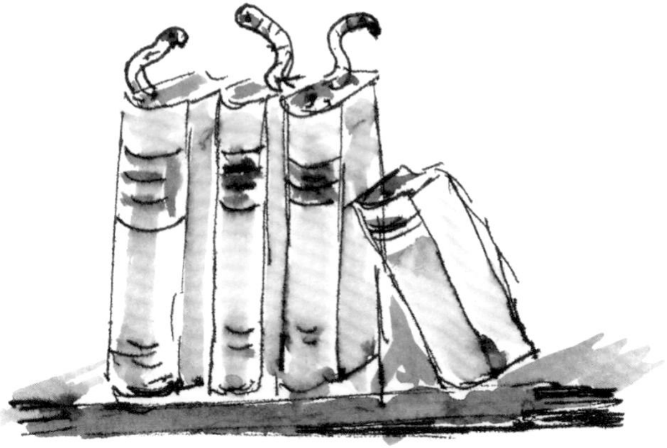

In mint condition –
second-hand books
flavoursome to bookworms

❖

Apple computer –
so many bytes
to crunch the data

❖

Computing

Mountain-top hotel
leaving my lap-top below
clearing the memory

⁘

Gazing out of Windows
not learning the language –
computer dyslexia

⁘

Adding megabytes
to computer memory –
wish it were my own

⁘

On the worldwide web
information overload
slipping through the net

❖

Cyberspace friend
a keystroke away
virtually real

❖

Computer virus
hacking cough
Microsoft tissues

❖

Sitting on my knee
my wife commandeers
my lap-top

❖

On my computer
life's a beach –
surfing, crashing

❖

"You've got mail" –
computer screen brightening
my face dims

❖

Travel –
broadening the mind
and my waistline

❖

On Vacation

Our vacation
snapped shut in the pages
of my photo album

❖

All those souvenirs –
bringing home
another world

❖

Future friends
reading the same
holiday brochure

❖

On top of the world
altitude sickness
feeling low

⁘

Travel brochures open –
our car-sick dog
hides

⁘

Jumbo jet
taking on board
my trunkful

⁘

Glazed stares
behind the windows
of the tour bus

⁘

Headphones and a book
ignoring the scenic route
teenage traveller

⁘

His castle in the air –
architect getting a stronghold
on a daydream

❖

Castle on the rocks
time and tide
waiting

❖

Cross-channel ferry
rough sea
car sick

❖

Slow car in front
not knowing
the going rate

❖

Footloose –
one step before
footsore

❖

Sandwich by the lake –
ducks always know
the best picnic spot

❖

Ducks and drakes
skimming over the lake –
just a stone's throw

❖

Station clock
above the silent track –
marking time

❖

Gnarled roots
matching the hands
of the old gardener

❖

Gardening

Careworn gardener
corduroy trousers
on their last legs

⁘

Leaning on the fence
planning growth –
garden politics

⁘

Herbal garden
blowing in the wind
aromatherapy

⁘

Tree surgeon
acrobat with chain saw
suburban monkey

⁘

Her new friend
the gardener –
the old rake

⁘

Overgrowth –
empty cottage
mourning its gardener

⁘

Lone pine
scattering cones
for another

⁘

Time and grass
wait for no man –
the constant gardener

⁘

Garden gnome
beneath the bird feeder –
on his head be it

⁘

Gardener's teatime –
planting herself
on the old oak bench

⁘

Taken by storm
roof tiles in flight –
birds grounded

⁘

Spring

Mad March hare
fooling about
in April

⁘

Easter gales
daffodils flattened –
poetic justice?

⁘

Cuckoos fall silent –
no-one stops to listen
to the second one

⁘

August 12th –
game birds
always grouse

❖

Summer

After an innings
cricketers stumping up
for another round

⁘

Bat on ball
tinkling ice
sounds of summer

⁘

Wimbledon finals –
ice-cream van
serving at full lick

⁘

Summer storm
lightning over the mountain
air of high tension

❖

Lightning strike
paralysing
the powerless

❖

Cottage industry –
gardens open
for charity

❖

Solar-powered
electric fence
cows stunned

❖

Cocktails for two
in a hammock for one –
gin sling

❖

Evening quiet
the distant roar
of a hot-air balloon

❖

Autumn

Hot-air balloon –
vertigo silencing
the chatterer

⁘

Letting go
at the end of life's work
autumn leaves

⁘

Autumn leaf fall
capturing the moment –
photo finish

⁘

Shotgun snapping shut –
to fly or not to fly
the pheasant decides

⁂

Pheasant wings whirring
shooters taking aim –
the game is up

⁂

Wood smoke –
the scent of autumn
hanging in the air

⁂

First evening chill
the spaniel lies
before the unlit fire

⁂

Autumn mist
mellow fruitfulness
wasps picnicking

❖

Stately home
sweeping lawns
the autumn gardener

❖

Mountain pine –
needles on the ground
sewing a carpet

❖

Roof gutter blocked
larch trees
giving me the needle

❖

High risk –
mountain pines
living on the edge

❖

Winter

Bare trees in December
skeletons in the wood
shivering their timbers

⁘

Frozen waterfall
waiting for springtime –
interrupted journey

⁘

Snow pigment falling
painting out familiar land –
monochrome beauty

⁘

Stalactite of ice
refracting brilliant sunshine –
once a drip

❖

Snow crystals
sitting on the fence
to melt or not to melt?

❖

Winter duvet
snuggled
down

❖

Tracks
in the snow
who goes there?

❖

Snowflakes
silently swirling –
heavenly ballet

❖

Low winter sun
my shadow
walking tall

⁘

Schnapps in their coffee
old friends warming up
their conviviality

⁘

Bracing weather –
snowdrops
drooping

⁘

Snowdrift
snow boots –
too short

⁘

Housebound –
winter looking in
at every window

⁂

Numb fingertips
feeling
winter's grip

⁂

No lawns to cut
his winter
of content

⁂

Woodland walk
snow on the bough
getting it in the neck

⁂

Silent night
cold marble floor
the mouse tiptoes

⁘

Christmas

Country walk
my friend the turkey
no longer there

⁘

Christmas Eve
children sleeping –
one eye open

⁘

My family
wrapping Christmas gifts –
string quartet

⁘

Christmas fare –
twice as much
as usual

⁘

Christmas turkey
we gobble
the gobbler

⁘

Mulled wine –
infusing me
with Yuletide spirit

⁘

Christmas wreath –
cigar smoke
spiralling

⁘

Festive season –
eating Stilton
getting portly

❖

Herded together –
sheepdog on a quad-bike
the balance of power

❖

Country Life

Tracking the tractor
blackbirds enjoying
a ploughman's lunch

⁘

Brussels sprouts –
European Union
Agricultural Policy

⁘

Village pub
pint-sized
hospitality

⁘

Village pub
locals at the bar
standing at ease

❖

In the Fox and Hounds
master at the bar
fireside mongrel dreaming

❖

Combine harvester
colossus of the fields
such neat packaging

❖

Her friend approaching
along the village street –
the spaniel sits

❖

Thatcher on the roof –
cottage garden
getting the short straw

❖

Country bus
reuniting friends
community pick-up

⁘

Stone-flagged floor
concave from signalling
the march of time

⁘

Sheep staring –
chewing over
my windstopper fleece

⁘

Horses whinnying
at our approach –
neighbourhood watch

⁘

Sheep-dip day
old ewe pulling the wool
over her eyes

✣

Farmers' Ball
red eye
in the morning

✣

Man-made woodland
in fine array –
so very spruce

✣

Fly fisherman
craftily casting
trick or treat

✣

New Year resolutions –
how trying
to keep

❖

New Year

New year
old me –
yet the optimist

❖

New Year's Day
power cut
cooking her goose

❖

Hogmanay reveller
first foot
which one?

❖

Yoga student
searching for tranquillity –
on her head be it

❖

Health Care

Getting abreast
of new technology –
silicone implant

✣

Chatting up
the surgery receptionist –
complimentary medicine

✣

Crowded waiting room
meeting old friends
and new viruses

✣

Mobile chiropodist –
footloose in search of
foot-faults

❖

Tinnitus –
not music
to my ears

❖

Private consultant
taking my illness
into his account

❖

Down in the mouth
then coming up smiling –
dental hygienist

❖

Keep off the grass –
government
health warning

❖

Aching to escape
from my osteopath's
backchat

❖

Cocktail sausages –
how will I get rid of
my fistful of sticks?

❖

My Party Face

Come to my party?
the prospect
less than inviting

❖

Powerless to leave
switching off –
my party face dims

❖

Too noisy to hear
too hoarse to speak
too polite to leave

❖

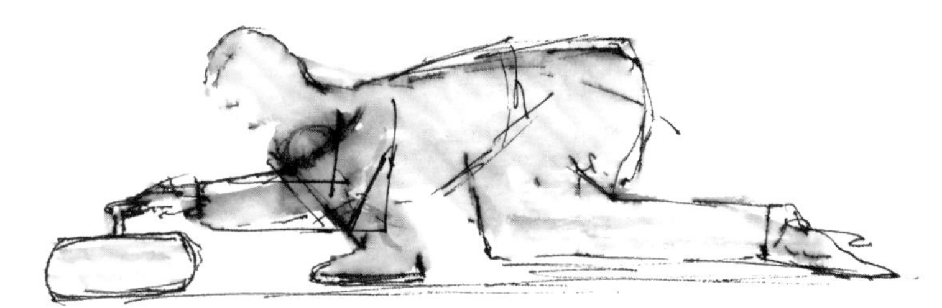

Granite resolve –
curling skip releasing
the deciding stone

⁘

Sport

Tennis final
my idol serves –
my nerve broken

❖

Commercial break
fast serve
to the couch potato

❖

Climbing friend of old
maps on the table –
some contours stay the same

❖

Tabloid headlines
every morning
in your face

❖

Family Life

Housewife
pumping
the iron

⁘

My wife
needing me twice
at the cash and carry

⁘

Silent woman
searching for the word –
oxymoron

⁘

Flaming red
her hair
beyond the pale

❖

Kitchen sink
making a drama
out of my turn

❖

Irritated housewife
not seeing me for dust
I return when it settles

❖

Taking a new recipe
off the kitchen shelf
cooking the books

❖

Country kitchen
scones on the griddle
aromatherapy

❖

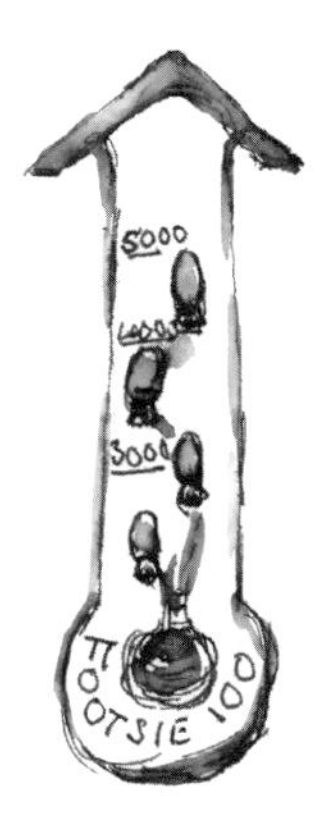

Wealthy widow –
her stockbroker
playing footsie

❖

Simmering in the kitchen
waiting to be appreciated
the chef and her stew

❖

Buying an old chair
from an antique dealer –
not a leg to stand on

❖

My solicitor
willing me
onward

❖

Busy telephone booth
I wait
at the gas station

❖

All my hot water –
making a clean breast of it
wife in the shower

❖

Dustbin rescue
favourite old sweater
a close-knit thing

❖

Gleeful boy
stone in hand –
the greenhouse effect

❖

A draggy day –
in tow
to the shops

❖

Our daughter eventing
her bedroom
the ungroomed

⁘

Crystal glass –
so transparently
expensive

⁘

Rhythm of the road
humming along
only the car in tune

❖

Motoring

In love with speed
fast car
hugging the road

⁘

Hairpin bend
four-wheel drive
getting a grip

⁘

Moorland road
two cars passing
forefingers saluting

⁘

Hedgehog
dodging
the road hog

⁘

Single-track road
only the scenery
passing by

⁘

Snow chains –
getting a grip
on going nowhere

⁘

Life's a drive
looking forward more than back
or you crash

❖

Anxious traveller
in a flurry –
of snow

❖

Driver's licence
freedom of the road
and the back seat

❖

Caribbean evening
a rum do –
I'll be jiggered

❖

Cheers

Bicycling
to the bottle bank –
for a longer life

⁘

Wine taster
spitting out
his opinion

⁘

A vintage year –
installing a stairlift
to the wine cellar

⁘

HAY LOFT
SO NOW DO YOU UNDERSTAND HAIKU?
THE END